PIRATES IN THE MEDIA

KENNY ABDO

Fly!
An Imprint of Abdo Zoom
abdobooks.com

abdobooks.com

Published by Abdo Zoom, a division of ABDO, P.O. Box 398166, Minneapolis, Minnesota 55439. Copyright © 2022 by Abdo Consulting Group, Inc. International copyrights reserved in all countries. No part of this book may be reproduced in any form without written permission from the publisher. Fly!™ is a trademark and logo of Abdo Zoom.

Printed in the United States of America, North Mankato, Minnesota.
102021
012022

Photo Credits: Alamy, AP Images, Everett Collection, Getty Images, Shutterstock
Production Contributors: Kenny Abdo, Jennie Forsberg, Grace Hansen
Design Contributors: Candice Keimig, Neil Klinepier, Laura Graphenteen

Library of Congress Control Number: 2021940192

Publisher's Cataloging-in-Publication Data

Names: Abdo, Kenny, author.
Title: Pirates in the media / by Kenny Abdo
Description: Minneapolis, Minnesota : Abdo Zoom, 2022 | Series: Pirates | Includes online resources and index.
Identifiers: ISBN 9781098226893 (lib. bdg.) | ISBN 9781644947043 (pbk.) | ISBN 9781098227739 (ebook) | ISBN 9781098228156 (Read-to-Me ebook)
Subjects: LCSH: Pirates--Juvenile literature. | Pirates in mass media--Juvenile literature. | Pirates in motion pictures--Juvenile literature. | Pirates--History--Juvenile literature. | Piracy--Juvenile literature.
Classification: DDC 910.4--dc23

Pirates in the Media 4

Ye Olde Yarn 8

Vast Bounty 12

Glossary 22

Online Resources 23

Index 24

PIRATES IN THE MEDIA

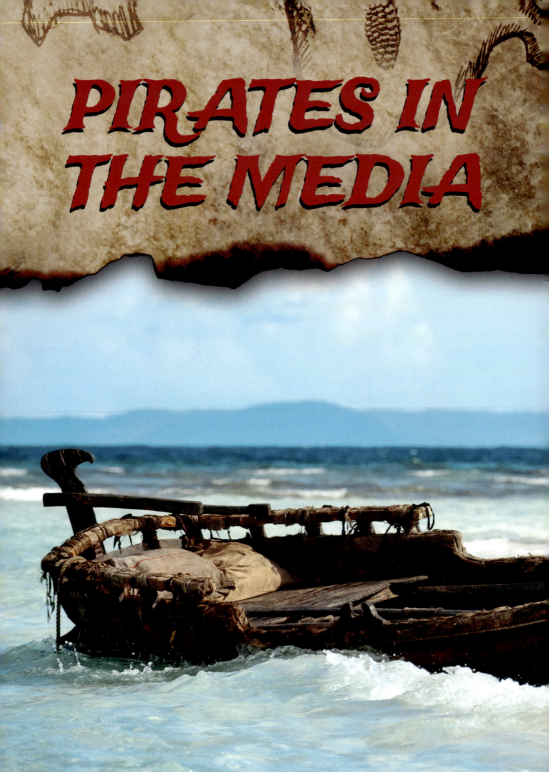

Once hard to capture, pirates are now all over today's media from books to TV shows!

Pirates in modern fiction are flashy and fun. However, they don't have much in common with the real-life buccaneers who sailed the seas so long ago!

YE OLDE YARN

Pirates have been invading popular culture for centuries. Published in 1719, *Robinson Crusoe* was one of the first **depictions** of **piracy** in literature.

From there, pirates swung from the pages to the stages. Then they ransacked TV screens and movie theaters around the world.

Pirates are popular **mascots** for sporting teams, too! The NFL's Tampa Bay Buccaneers and Las Vegas Raiders both sport pirate imagery in their logos.

VAST BOUNTY

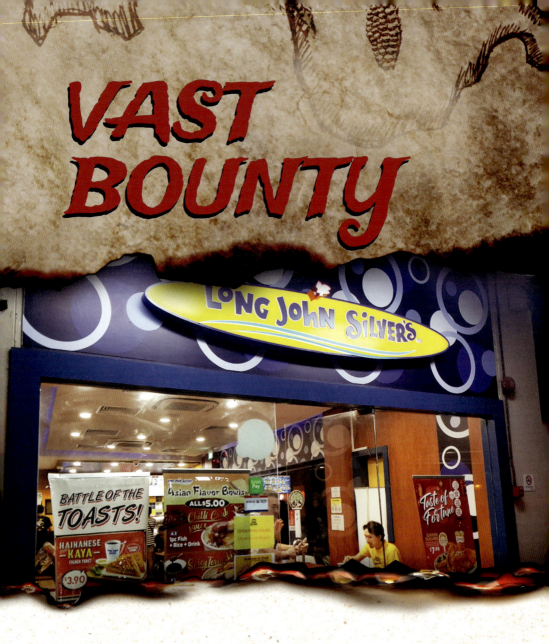

Treasure Island debuted in 1882. It introduced the world to Long John Silver. He was so popular that Silver had a national restaurant **chain** named after him in 1969.

The Pittsburg Pirates date back to 1891, making them one of the oldest baseball teams in history. Known for poaching other teams' best players, they were often called "piratical."

Captain Hook made his first appearance in the play *Peter Pan* in 1904. He has appeared in just about everything related to Peter Pan ever since, including movies, books, and cartoons.

One-Eyed Willie and his hidden **loot** drove the plot in *The Goonies*. Generations of fans enjoyed watching Mikey and the gang search for the precious treasure.

Will Turner, Jack Sparrow, and Elizabeth Swann captained the *Pirates of the Caribbean* **franchise**! Turner was a blacksmith who eventually became captain of the Flying Dutchman.

Premiering in 2011, *Jake and the Never Land Pirates* was a TV treasure! The show followed Jake and his **mates** as they battled Captain Hook for riches. It lasted 116 episodes!

Barkhad Abdi, a first-time actor starred in the 2013 film *Captain Phillips*. His portrayal of real-life pirate Abduwali Muse was so scary and believable, that Abdi was nominated for an **Oscar**!

Pirates of old were ruthless and mean. But the fictional characters they created had a cultural influence worth tons of gold.

GLOSSARY

chain – a restaurant that has many locations.

depict – to describe something through drawing, photographs, or other art forms.

franchise – a collection of related movies in a series.

loot – stolen goods and treasure.

mascot – a character or thing that brings good luck and helps cheer on a team.

mate – a fellow member of a ship's crew.

Oscar – one of several awards the Academy of Motion Picture Arts and Sciences gives to the best actors and filmmakers of the year.

piracy – the practice of attacking and robbing ships at sea.

ONLINE RESOURCES

Booklinks
NONFICTION NETWORK
FREE! ONLINE NONFICTION RESOURCES

To learn more about Pirates in the Media, please visit abdobooklinks.com or scan this QR code. These links are routinely monitored and updated to provide the most current information available.

23

INDEX

Abdi, Barkhad 20

Buccaneers (team) 11

Captain Hook 15, 18

Captain Phillips (movie) 20

Goonies, The (movie) 16

Jake and the Never Land Pirates (TV show) 18

Long John Silver 12

One-Eyed Willie 16

Peter Pan (series) 15

Pirates (team) 14

Pirates of the Caribbean (series) 17

Raiders (team) 11

Robinson Crusoe (book) 8

Treasure Island (book) 12